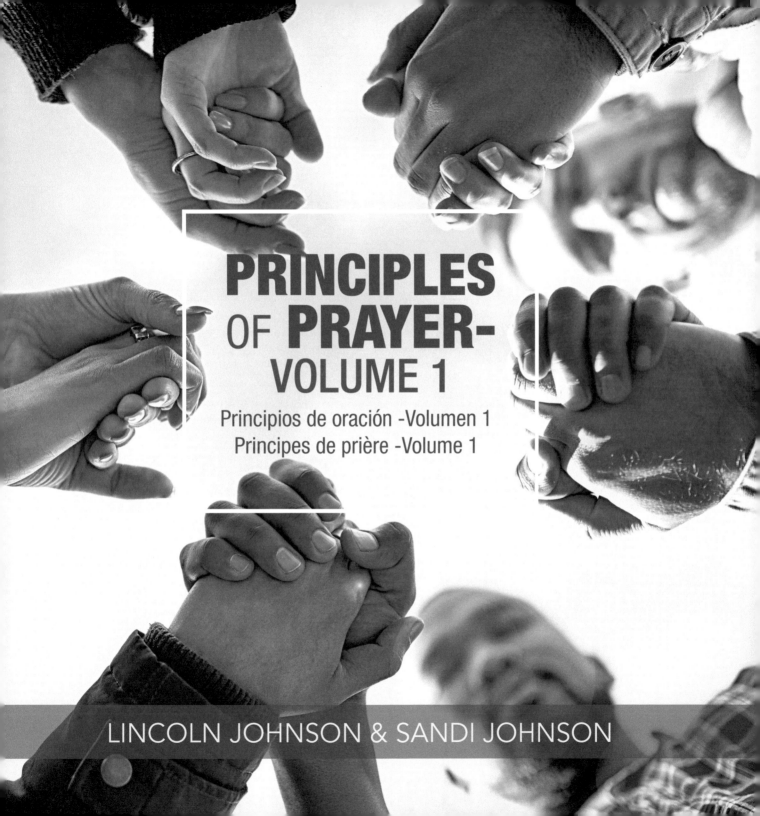

PRINCIPLES OF **PRAYER**- VOLUME 1

Principios de oración -Volumen 1
Principes de prière -Volume 1

LINCOLN JOHNSON & SANDI JOHNSON

Order this book online at www.trafford.com
or email orders@trafford.com

Most Trafford titles are also available at major online book retailers.

Trafford www.trafford.com
PUBLISHING®
North America & international
toll-free: 1 888 232 4444 (USA & Canada)
fax: 812 355 4082

Our mission is to efficiently provide the world's finest, most comprehensive book publishing service, enabling every author to experience success. To find out how to publish your book, your way, and have it available worldwide, visit us online at www.trafford.com

Scripture quotations marked KJV are from the Holy Bible, King James Version (Authorized Version). First published in 1611. Quoted from the KJV Classic Reference Bible, Copyright © 1983 by The Zondervan Corporation.

ISBN: 978-1-4907-9961-2 (sc)

ISBN: 978-1-4907-9962-9 (e)

Print information available on the last page.

Trafford rev. 02/12/2020

PRINCIPLES OF PRAYER-
VOLUME 1

This book is dedicated to the memories of Tom Cameron, Ralph Della Ratta, and Reverend F. Scott Teets. These three men were instrumental to our early stages of growth and maturity in the faith for both Sandi and I.

Principles of prayer -Volume 1

by Lincoln & Sandi Johnson

ENGLISH
VERSION

Foreword:

In these last closing days, we live in a very complex world system. It is a world and a time where humans are overshadowed with the cares of this world. It is a time where our time, thoughts and innovative ideas are being replaced from the simplicity of life. It is very easy to forget how and when to communicate with God.

Has God heard my prayers and how should I pray? In this very inspirational and biblical points to prayer, Lincoln & Sandi Johnson gives us some very fruitful biblical nuggets of wisdom in relation to God's principles of prayer. These five prayer points are powerful, inspirational and cogent but at the same time, simple for the everyday reader.

Lincoln & Sandi Johnson fastidiously digs deep into the biblical accounts of prayer. They provide the relative scriptural evidence and references to push their points home. According to Jesus, it is what we do in secret that matters the most. This simple yet robust biblical teaching on prayer, gives the reader many examples from the mouth of Jesus Christ Himself as it relates to prayer.

It also gives us clear examples of the early Christian church, pointing us to prayer practices that pleases God. Would to God that we as postmodern Christians realise the key to God's heart through the beautiful language of prayer. We are not drawn to perfunctory prayer but meaningful prayer. It is not done out of religious obligation, but by the desires of our heart and absolute love for God and His blessed son Jesus Christ, our Lord and Saviour, who is GOD.

I absolutely recommend this write up on the principles of prayer.

For Direct Enquires please contact
Pastor. Dr. A.E. Christopher
**Rightly Dividing the Word Ministry &
School of Theology**

Principal and Dean of Academic Affairs
For Direct Enquires please contact
Email 1 - dr.christopher@aocf.org.uk
Email 2 - achrist109@aol.com

Mob - 07448169768

Also In association with…
Alpha & Omega Christian Fellowship
Room H, 1 Tower Lane, Business Park
East Lane, North Wembley Middx HA9 7NB

Tel: +44 0208 908 1337
Email: info@aocf.org.uk
Website: www.aocf.org.uk

Principle 1.
Prayer must be taught (Luke 11:1).

We are often quick to remind believers to pray about a situation they might face while assuming that they know how to pray. Like most disciplines, prayer is one that requires development and practice and therefore, teaching is needed. Jesus said after this manner, pray (see Matthew 6:9 & Luke 11:2). In other words, pray using this framework:

• Our Father which art in heaven, hallowed be Thy Name. Thy kingdom come. Thy will be done in earth, as it is in heaven.

As God's children, we have a heavenly father, to Whom we can go to. It identifies Who is our source. God is holy and His Name is to be revered. His kingdom and His will are carried out, and is manifested in our lives as citizens of the heavenly kingdom displayed as pilgrims here on the earth.

• Give us day by day our daily bread (Luke 11:3).

We are to pray and give thanks to God for all our daily blessings and benefits. Praying in this manner show our trust in Him as our sole provider. That He's concerned about the needs of His children as a good Father.

• And forgive us our sins; for we also forgive every one that is indebted to us. And lead us not into temptation; but deliver us from evil (Luke 11: 4).

As God forgive us of our sins and set us free. So are we to extend forgiveness to those who have done us wrong-releasing them so that we can be free. God will give us direction, leading us away from temptation. As our provider, we can trust Him to lead us away from temptation and to preserve our lives from evil.

• ...For thine is the kingdom, and the power, and the glory, forever. Amen (Matthew 6:13)

Jesus is the king of His Kingdom. When you think about the Kingdom of God, what should be apparent is that Jesus is the head of His spiritual kingdom, the Church. He is the sovereign ruler that extends mercy and grace to all His citizens. Furthermore, life is more manageable when we can cast all our cares upon the Lord because He cares for us-and besides, He has all power in heaven and in the earth.

Principle 2.
All prayer must be done in The Name of Jesus (John 14:12-14, 16:23-24, John 5:43 and Colossians 3:17).

The use and application of the Name of Jesus in prayer guarantees results. In John, chapter 14, Jesus told His disciples that he that believes in Him, will do the same works that He did also; and greater works shall the believers do after Jesus ascended.

And whatever we ask in Jesus' Name, He will do it! We as believers do all in The Name of Jesus; this includes all prayers.

Principle 3.
All prayer must be subjected to The Lord's will: (I Corinthians 4:19, James 4:15, 1 John 5:14-15)

Whenever prayer is made, it must be done according to God's will. The Bible tells us in Isaiah 55:8 (KJV) that "For my thoughts are not your thoughts, neither are your ways my ways."

Oftentimes when we pray for someone, though our intentions for them may be good, it may not be what the will of God is for that individual-especially, if that person is gravely ill and it is God's will to lay them to rest. We don't want to pray and speak presumptuously and say that God will raise you up from this bed of affliction when He did not say so. This action can cause someone to lose trust in the Lord and discourage family members, friends, and even acquaintances. God does not go against His Will!

We have confidence in God that if we ask anything according to His will, He hears us. And if we know that He hears us, whatsoever we ask, we know that we have the requests that we desired of Him. 2 John 5:15 (KJV).

Principle 4.
Fasting and Prayer (Daniel 9:3; Matthew 17:21; Mark 9:29, Acts 14:23).

For urgent needs of great importance or significance, fasting must be accompanied with prayer. Fasting, like prayer, is an expected discipline found in both the Old and New Testament. When an individual fast, he/she is crucifying the flesh and dying out to selfish ambitions, pride, lust, and/or any obstacles that clouds our thinking and spiritual vision. Our spiritual senses are sharpened when we are engaged in fasting and the result is a more intimate relationship with the Lord Jesus.

Jesus told his disciples in Matthew 6:16,
when you fast, be not as the hypocrites, of a sad countenance, but carry out your usual activities for daily living. In other words, wash your face and brush your teeth, and dress yourself as you would on any other day so as not to appear like you are fasting. Fast in secret unto the Lord who will reward you openly!
After that we have fasted and prayed, especially for any extended days, we are humbled, and our spiritual senses are keener as we are more sensitive to the Holy Spirit that resides in us as true believers.

Principle 5.
Praying in the Spirit (Romans 8:26 and Jude 20).

To many people, praying in the Spirit may mean different things. However, one thing is certain, one must have the Spirit to pray in Spirit. In John 14:16-17, Jesus told the disciples that He would pray to the Father and He would give them another Comforter, that may abide with His disciples forever. In other words, the Spirit of Truth, whom the world cannot receive, because it sees Him not, neither know Him, but His disciples know Him, for He dwells with them, and shall be in them.

Moreover, Romans 8:9 unambiguously stated that anyone that does not have the Spirit (Holy Ghost), they are none of His. Moreover, in John 3:5, Jesus told Nicodemus that he must be born of the water and of the Spirit to enter in the kingdom of God. Secondly, in John 4:23-24, Jesus in His conversation with the Samaritan woman at the well, told her that the Father seeks to be worshipped in Spirit and in truth. Moreover, because God is a Spirit, they that worship Him, must worship Him in spirit and in truth.

For as many as are led by the Spirit of God, they are the sons of God...............For you have received the Spirit of adoption, whereby you cry Abba, Father. The Spirit itself bears witness with our spirit, that we are the children of God. Romans 8:14, Romans 8:15, Galatians 4:5-6

Likewise, the Spirit also helps our illnesses, for we don't know what we should pray for as we should, but the Spirit itself makes intercession for us with groanings which cannot be uttered. And He that searches the hearts knows what the mind of the Spirit is because He makes intercession for the saints according to the will of God (Romans 8: 26-27). Praying in the Spirit, gives the believer the opportunity and access to the only one, who can provide, bless, heal and save. We can rest assured, that God not only hears, but we are confident that He will answer. Whatever the answer is, whether it is yes or no, we will have His peace.

Although these five principles are not an exhaustive application of prayer, our prayer is that these five principles will help you establish a strong daily life of prayer that is grounded in the framework of prayer taught by the scriptures. All prayer must be in faith towards God acknowledging who you are praying to. All prayer must acknowledge Jesus so that the Father may be glorified in the Son. John 14:13-14 says, whatsoever you ask in my name, that will I do, that the Father may be glorified in the Son. If you shall ask anything in my name, I will do it! Communication (prayer) with God needs to be a part of our lifestyle. So, we need to engage in prayer daily. When a person communicates, they alternate between listening and speaking. So too should prayer be, as we communicate with God.

When you pray, begin with praise while acknowledging your heavenly Father. Secondly, repent for known and unknown sins and/or faults. When we confess our sins to the Lord, our advocate, we are taking ownership for our actions while admitting our need and dependency on the Lord. Third, our time of prayer should include supplications for others. When we consider how many people we know from our relatives, friends, acquaintances, neighbors, co-workers, there are a lot of people and their needs to pray for especially their salvation. Fourth, we should pray to be used as a witness daily, in addition to praying for our specific needs and the areas in our lives that we need the lord's help. Lastly, we need to express our gratitude to the Lord before closing out our prayer in Jesus' name.

We would be remiss if we did not share with you the Gospel message of being born again. In John Chapter 3, verses 1-8, Jesus shared the principle for being born again. The disciple Luke gave us four witnesses to become born again; Acts 2:37-39, Acts 8:12-17, Acts 10.

SPANISH
VERSION

Este livro é dedicado às memórias de Tom Cameron, Ralph Della Ratta e Reverendo F. Scott Teets. Esses três homens foram fundamentais para nossos estágios iniciais de crescimento e maturidade na fé, tanto para Sandi quanto para eu.

Principios de oración -Volumen 1

de Lincoln & Sandi Johnson

El Prefacio:

En estos últimos días de cierre, vivimos en un sistema mundial muy complejo. Es un mundo y una época en la que los humanos se ven ensombrecidos por las preocupaciones de este mundo. Es un momento en el que nuestro tiempo, pensamientos e ideas innovadoras están siendo reemplazados por la simplicidad de la vida. Es muy fácil olvidar cómo y cuándo comunicarse con Dios.

¿Dios ha escuchado mis oraciones y cómo debo orar? En estos puntos muy inspiradores y bíblicos para la oración, Lincoln y Sandi Johnson nos dan algunas pepitas bíblicas de sabiduría muy fructíferas en relación con los principios de oración de Dios. Estos cinco puntos de oración son poderosos, inspiradores y convincentes, pero al mismo tiempo, simples para el lector cotidiano.

Lincoln y Sandi Johnson cavan profundamente en los relatos bíblicos de la oración. Proporcionan la evidencia bíblica relativa y referencias para llevar sus puntos a casa. Según Jesús, lo que hacemos en secreto es lo que más importa. Esta enseñanza bíblica simple pero sólida sobre la oración, le da al lector muchos ejemplos de la boca de Jesucristo mismo en relación con la oración.

También nos da ejemplos claros de la iglesia cristiana primitiva, y nos señala prácticas de oración que agradan a Dios. Ojalá que nosotros, como cristianos posmodernos, nos demos cuenta de la clave del corazón de Dios a través del hermoso lenguaje de la oración. No nos atrae la oración superficial, sino la oración significativa. No se hace por obligación religiosa, sino por los deseos de nuestro corazón y el amor absoluto por Dios y su bendito hijo Jesucristo, nuestro Señor y Salvador, quien es DIOS.

Recomiendo absolutamente este artículo sobre los principios de la oración.

Para consultas diretas, entre em contato
Pastor Dr. A.E. Christopher
Dividir corretamente a Palavra Ministério e
Escola de Teologia

Diretor e Decano de Assuntos Acadêmicos
Para consultas diretas, entre em contato
Email 1 - dr.christopher@aocf.org.uk
Email 2 - achrist109@aol.com

Mob - 07448169768

Também em associação com ...
Alfa & Omega Christian Fellowship
Quarto H, 1 Tower Lane, Business Park
East Lane, Wembley do Norte Middx HA9 7NB

Tel: +44 0208 908 1337
E-mail: info@aocf.org.uk
Website: www.aocf.org.uk

Princípio 1
A oração deve ser ensinada (Lucas 11: 1).

Muitas vezes, somos rápidos em lembrar os crentes a orarem sobre uma situação que possam enfrentar, ao assumir que sabem orar. Como a maioria das disciplinas, a oração exige desenvolvimento e prática e, portanto, é necessário ensinar. Jesus disse assim: ore (veja Mateo 6: 9 e Lucas 11: 2). Em outras palavras, ore usando esta estrutura:

• Pai nosso que estás nos céus, santificado seja o teu nome. Teu reino come. Seja feita a tua vontade na terra, como no céu.

Como filhos de Deus, temos um pai celestial, a quem podemos ir. Ele identifica quem é a nossa fonte. Deus é santo e Seu nome deve ser reverenciado. Seu reino e Sua vontade são realizados e se manifestam em nossas vidas como cidadãos do reino celestial, exibidos como peregrinos aqui na terra.

• Dê-nos dia a dia o nosso pão diário (Lucas 11: 3).

Devemos orar e dar graças a Deus por todas as nossas bênçãos e benefícios diários. Orar dessa maneira mostra nossa confiança nEle como nosso único provedor. Que Ele está preocupado com as necessidades de Seus filhos como um bom Pai.

• E perdoa-nos os nossos pecados; pois também perdoamos todo aquele que é devedor de nós. E não nos deixe cair em tentação; mas livrai-nos do mal (Lucas 11: 4).

Como Deus nos perdoa nossos pecados e nos liberta. Assim devemos estender o perdão àqueles que nos fizeram libertá-los de maneira errada, para que possamos ser livres. Deus nos dará direção, afastando-nos da tentação. Como nosso provedor, podemos confiar nEle para nos afastar da tentação e preservar nossa vida do mal.

• ... Pois teu é o reino, e o poder, e a glória, para sempre. Amém (Mateus 6: 13b)

Jesus é o rei do seu reino. Quando você pensa sobre o Reino de Deus, o que deveria ser aparente é que Jesus é a cabeça de Seu reino espiritual, a Igreja. Ele é o governante soberano que concede misericórdia e graça a todos os seus cidadãos. Além disso, a vida é mais administrável quando podemos lançar todos os nossos cuidados sobre o Senhor, porque Ele se importa conosco - e além disso, Ele tem todo o poder no céu e na terra.

Princípio 2
Toda oração deve ser feita em O Nome de Jesus (João 14: 12-14, 16: 23-24, João 5:43 e Colossenses 3:17).

O uso e aplicação do Nome de Jesus na oração garante resultados. Em João, capítulo 14, Jesus disse a Seus discípulos que aquele que nEle crê, fará as mesmas obras que Ele também; e obras maiores os crentes farão depois que Jesus ascender.

E tudo o que pedirmos em nome de Jesus, Ele fará! Nós, como crentes, fazemos tudo em O Nome de Jesus; Isso inclui todas as orações.

Principio 3.
Toda oración debe estar sujeta a la voluntad del Señor: (1 Corintios 4:19, Santiago 4:15, 1 Juan 5: 14-15)

Cada vez que se hace una oración, debe hacerse de acuerdo con la voluntad de Dios. La Biblia nos dice en Isaías 55: 8 (RV) que "Porque mis pensamientos no son tus pensamientos, ni tus caminos son mis caminos".

A menudo, cuando oramos por alguien, aunque nuestras intenciones para con él pueden ser buenas, puede que no sea la voluntad de Dios para ese individuo, especialmente si esa persona está gravemente enferma y es la voluntad de Dios ponerla a descansar. No queremos orar y hablar presuntuosamente y decir que Dios te levantará de este lecho de aflicción cuando no lo dijo. Esta acción puede hacer que alguien pierda la confianza en el Señor y desanime a los miembros de la familia, amigos e incluso conocidos. ¡Dios no va en contra de su voluntad!

Tenemos confianza en Dios de que si le pedimos algo de acuerdo a su voluntad, Él nos escucha. Y si sabemos que Él nos escucha, cualquier cosa que le pidamos, sabemos que tenemos las peticiones que deseamos de Él. 2 Juan 5:15 (KJV).

Principio 4.
Ayuno y oración (Daniel 9: 3; Mateo 17:21; Marcos 9:29, Hechos 14:23).

Para necesidades urgentes de gran importancia o importancia, el ayuno debe ir acompañado de oración. El ayuno, como la oración, es una disciplina esperada que se encuentra tanto en el Antiguo como en el Nuevo Testamento. Cuando un individuo ayuna, él / ella está crucificando la carne y muriendo a ambiciones egoístas, orgullo, lujuria y / o cualquier obstáculo que nubla nuestro pensamiento y visión espiritual. Nuestros sentidos espirituales se agudizan cuando nos dedicamos al ayuno y el resultado es una relación más íntima con el Señor Jesús.

Jesús les dijo a sus discípulos en Mateo 6:16:
cuando ayunas, no seas como los hipócritas, de semblante triste, sino realiza tus actividades habituales para la vida diaria. En otras palabras, lávate la cara y cepíllate los dientes, y vístete como lo harías cualquier otro día para no parecer que estás ayunando. ¡Ayune en secreto al Señor que lo recompensará abiertamente!

Después de eso, hemos ayunado y orado, especialmente durante cualquier día prolongado, nos sentimos humildes y nuestros sentidos espirituales son más agudos, ya que somos más sensibles al Espíritu Santo que reside en nosotros como verdaderos creyentes.

Principio 5.
Orando en el Espíritu (Romanos 8:26 y Judas 20).

Para muchas personas, orar en el Espíritu puede significar cosas diferentes. Sin embargo, una cosa es cierta, uno debe tener el Espíritu para orar en Espíritu. En Juan 14: 16-17, Jesús les dijo a los discípulos que oraría al Padre y que les daría otro Consolador, que podría permanecer con Sus discípulos para siempre. En otras palabras, el Espíritu de la Verdad, a quien el mundo no puede recibir, porque no lo ve, ni lo conoce, sino que Sus discípulos lo conocen, porque Él habita con ellos y estará en ellos.

Además, Romanos 8: 9 declaró inequívocamente que cualquiera que no tenga el Espíritu (Espíritu Santo), no es de los suyos. Además, en Juan 3: 5, Jesús le dijo a Nicodemo que debía nacer del agua y del Espíritu para entrar en el reino de Dios. En segundo lugar, en Juan 4: 23-24, Jesús, en su conversación con la mujer samaritana en el pozo, le dijo que el Padre busca ser adorado en Espíritu y en verdad. Además, como Dios es un Espíritu, los que lo adoran deben adorarlo en espíritu y en verdad.

Para todos los que son guiados por el Espíritu de Dios, ellos son los hijos de Dios .... Porque ustedes han recibido el Espíritu de adopción, por el cual claman a Abba, Padre. El Espíritu mismo da testimonio a nuestro espíritu de que somos hijos de Dios. Romanos 8:14, Romanos 8:15, Gálatas 4: 5-6

Del mismo modo, el Espíritu también ayuda a nuestras enfermedades, porque no sabemos por qué debemos orar como deberíamos, pero el Espíritu mismo intercede por nosotros con gemidos que no se pueden pronunciar. Y el que busca en los corazones sabe cuál es la mente del Espíritu porque intercede por los santos según la voluntad de Dios (Romanos 8: 26-27). Orar en el Espíritu, le da al creyente la oportunidad y el acceso al único, que puede proporcionar, bendecir, sanar y salvar. Podemos estar seguros de que Dios no solo escucha, sino que confiamos en que responderá. Cualquiera sea la respuesta, ya sea sí o no, tendremos Su paz.

Aunque estos cinco principios no son una aplicación exhaustiva de la oración, nuestra oración es que estos cinco principios lo ayudarán a establecer una vida diaria de oración fuerte que se basa en el marco de la oración que enseñan las Escrituras. Toda oración debe ser en fe hacia Dios reconociendo a quién le rezas. Toda oración debe reconocer a Jesús para que el Padre pueda ser glorificado en el Hijo. Juan 14: 13-14 dice, todo lo que pidas en mi nombre, eso haré, para que el Padre sea glorificado en el Hijo. Si preguntas algo en mi nombre, ¡lo haré! La comunicación (oración) con Dios debe ser parte de nuestro estilo de vida. Entonces, necesitamos participar en la oración diariamente. Cuando una persona se comunica, alterna entre escuchar y hablar. Así también debería ser la oración, ya que nos comunicamos con Dios.

Cuando ores, comienza con alabanzas mientras reconoces a tu Padre celestial. En segundo lugar, arrepiéntete por los pecados y /o fallas conocidas y desconocidas. Cuando confesamos nuestros pecados al Señor, nuestro defensor, tomamos posesión de nuestras acciones mientras admitimos nuestra necesidad y dependencia del Señor. Tercero, nuestro tiempo de oración debe incluir súplicas para otros. Cuando consideramos cuántas personas conocemos de nuestros parientes, amigos, conocidos, vecinos, compañeros de trabajo, hay muchas personas y sus necesidades de orar, especialmente por su salvación. Cuarto, debemos rezar para ser usados como testigos diariamente, además de orar por nuestras necesidades específicas y las áreas en nuestras vidas en las que necesitamos la ayuda del Señor. Por último, necesitamos expresar nuestra gratitud al Señor antes de cerrar nuestra oración en el nombre de Jesús.

Seríamos negligentes si no compartiéramos el mensaje del Evangelio de nacer de nuevo. En Juan Capítulo 3, versículos 1-8, Jesús compartió el principio de nacer de nuevo. El discípulo Lucas nos dio cuatro testigos para nacer de nuevo; Hechos 2: 37-39, Hechos 8: 12-17, Hechos 10.

FRENCH
VERSION

Ce livre est dédié aux souvenirs de Tom Cameron, Ralph Della Ratta et Révérend F. Scott Teets. Ces trois hommes ont contribué à nos premiers stades de croissance et de maturité dans la foi pour Sandi et moi.

Principes de prière -Volume 1

par Lincoln & Sandi Johnson

Préface:

En ces derniers jours de fermeture, nous vivons dans un système mondial très complexe. C'est un monde et un temps où les humains sont éclipsés par les soucis de ce monde. C'est un temps où notre temps, nos pensées et nos idées innovantes sont remplacées par la simplicité de la vie. Il est très facile d'oublier comment et quand communiquer avec Dieu.

Dieu a-t-il entendu mes prières et comment dois-je prier? Dans ces points très inspirants et bibliques de la prière, Lincoln & Sandi Johnson nous donne quelques pépites bibliques très fructueuses de sagesse en relation avec les principes de prière de Dieu. Ces cinq points de prière sont puissants, inspirants et convaincants mais en même temps, simples pour le lecteur de tous les jours.

Lincoln et Sandi Johnson approfondissent minutieusement les récits bibliques de la prière. Ils fournissent la preuve scripturaire relative et les références pour pousser leurs points de vue. Selon Jésus, c'est ce que nous faisons en secret qui compte le plus. Cet enseignement biblique simple mais robuste sur la prière, donne au lecteur de nombreux exemples de la bouche de Jésus-Christ lui-même en ce qui concerne la prière.

Il nous donne également des exemples clairs de l'Église chrétienne primitive, nous montrant des pratiques de prière qui plaisent à Dieu. Voudrait Dieu que nous, chrétiens postmodernes, réalisions la clé du cœur de Dieu à travers le beau langage de la prière. Nous ne sommes pas attirés par la prière superficielle mais par une prière significative. Cela ne se fait pas par obligation religieuse, mais par les désirs de notre cœur et l'amour absolu pour Dieu et son fils béni Jésus-Christ, notre Seigneur et Sauveur, qui est DIEU.

Je recommande absolument cet article sur les principes de la prière.

Pour les demandes directes, veuillez contacter
Pasteur. Dr A.E. Christopher
Diviser correctement le mot ministère et
École de théologie

Directeur et doyen des affaires académiques
Pour les demandes directes, veuillez contacter
Courriel 1 - dr.christopher@aocf.org.uk
Courriel 2 - achrist109@aol.com

Mob - 07448169768

Aussi en association avec…
Bourse chrétienne Alpha et Omega
Salle H, 1 Tower Lane, Business Park
East Lane, North Wembley Middx HA9 7NB

Tél: +44 0208 908 1337
Courriel: info@aocf.org.uk
Site Web: www.aocf.org.uk

Principe 1.
La prière doit être enseignée (Luc 11: 1).

Nous sommes souvent prompts à rappeler aux croyants de prier sur une situation à laquelle ils pourraient être confrontés tout en supposant qu'ils savent comment prier. Comme la plupart des disciplines, la prière est celle qui nécessite du développement et de la pratique et par conséquent, l'enseignement est nécessaire. Jésus a dit de cette manière, priez (voir Matthieu 6: 9 et Luc 11: 2). En d'autres termes, priez en utilisant ce cadre:

• Notre Père qui es aux cieux, que ton nom soit sanctifié. Que ton royaume vienne. Que ta volonté soit faite sur la terre comme au ciel.

En tant qu'enfants de Dieu, nous avons un père céleste, vers qui nous pouvons aller. Il identifie qui est notre source. Dieu est saint et son nom doit être vénéré. Son royaume et sa volonté se réalisent et se manifestent dans nos vies de citoyens du royaume céleste montrés comme des pèlerins ici sur la terre.

• Donnez-nous chaque jour notre pain quotidien (Luc 11: 3).

Nous devons prier et remercier Dieu pour toutes nos bénédictions et avantages quotidiens. Prier de cette manière montre notre confiance en Lui comme notre unique pourvoyeur. Qu'Il est préoccupé par les besoins de Ses enfants en tant que bon Père.

• Et pardonne-nous nos péchés; car nous pardonnons aussi à tous ceux qui nous sont redevables. Et ne nous soumet pas à la tentation; mais délivre-nous du mal (Luc 11: 4).

Comme Dieu nous pardonne nos péchés et nous libère. Nous devons donc étendre le pardon à ceux qui nous ont fait du mal en les libérant afin que nous puissions être libres. Dieu nous donnera une direction, nous éloignant de la tentation. En tant que pourvoyeur, nous pouvons lui faire confiance pour nous éloigner de la tentation et pour préserver notre vie du mal.

• ... Car à toi appartient le royaume, la puissance et la gloire pour toujours. Amen (Matthieu 6: 13b)

Jésus est le roi de son royaume. Lorsque vous pensez au Royaume de Dieu, ce qui devrait être évident, c'est que Jésus est le chef de Son royaume spirituel, l'Église. Il est le souverain souverain qui accorde miséricorde et grâce à tous ses citoyens. De plus, la vie est plus facile à gérer lorsque nous pouvons porter tous nos soucis sur le Seigneur parce qu'Il prend soin de nous - et en plus, Il a tout pouvoir au ciel et sur la terre.

Principe 2.
Toute prière doit être faite au Nom de Jésus (Jean 14: 12-14, 16: 23-24, Jean 5:43 et Colossiens 3:17).

L'utilisation et l'application du Nom de Jésus dans la prière garantissent des résultats. Dans Jean, chapitre 14, Jésus a dit à ses disciples que celui qui croit en lui fera les mêmes oeuvres qu'Il a faites aussi; et de plus grandes oeuvres les croyants feront après l'ascension de Jésus.

Et quoi que nous demandions au Nom de Jésus, Il le fera! En tant que croyants, nous faisons tout au Nom de Jésus; cela inclut toutes les prières.

Principe 3.
Toute prière doit être soumise à la volonté du Seigneur: (I Corinthiens 4:19, Jacques 4:15, 1 Jean 5: 14-15)

Chaque fois que la prière est faite, elle doit être faite selon la volonté de Dieu. La Bible nous dit dans Ésaïe 55: 8 (LSG) que «Car mes pensées ne sont pas vos pensées, ni vos voies mes voies.»

Souvent, lorsque nous prions pour quelqu'un, bien que nos intentions à son égard soient bonnes, il se peut que ce ne soit pas la volonté de Dieu pour cet individu, en particulier si cette personne est gravement malade et que Dieu a la volonté de la reposer. Nous ne voulons pas prier et parler avec présomption et dire que Dieu vous ressuscitera de ce lit d'affliction quand Il ne l'a pas dit. Cette action peut faire perdre à quelqu'un confiance dans le Seigneur et décourager les membres de la famille, les amis et même les connaissances. Dieu ne va pas contre sa volonté!

Nous avons confiance en Dieu que si nous demandons quelque chose selon sa volonté, il nous entend. Et si nous savons qu'il nous entend, quoi que nous demandions, nous savons que nous avons les demandes que nous souhaitions de lui. 2 Jean 5:15 (LSG).

Principe 4.
Jeûne et prière (Daniel 9: 3; Matthieu 17:21; Marc 9:29, Actes 14:23).

Pour les besoins urgents d'une grande importance ou signification, le jeûne doit être accompagné de la prière. Le jeûne, comme la prière, est une discipline attendue dans l'Ancien et le Nouveau Testament. Lorsqu'un individu jeûne, il / elle crucifie la chair et meurt aux ambitions égoïstes, à la fierté, à la luxure et / ou à tout obstacle qui obscurcit notre pensée et notre vision spirituelle. Nos sens spirituels sont aiguisés lorsque nous sommes engagés dans le jeûne et le résultat est une relation plus intime avec le Seigneur Jésus.

Jésus a dit à ses disciples dans Matthieu 6:16,
lorsque vous jeûnez, ne soyez pas comme les hypocrites, d'un visage triste, mais exercez vos activités habituelles pour la vie quotidienne. En d'autres termes, lavez-vous le visage et brossez-vous les dents, et habillez-vous comme vous le feriez un autre jour pour ne pas apparaître comme si vous jeûniez. Jeûnez en secret au Seigneur qui vous récompensera ouvertement!

Après cela, nous avons jeûné et prié, en particulier pendant des jours prolongés, nous sommes humiliés et nos sens spirituels sont plus vifs car nous sommes plus sensibles au Saint-Esprit qui réside en nous en tant que vrais croyants.

Principe 5.
Prier dans l'Esprit (Romains 8:26 et Jude 20).

Pour beaucoup de gens, prier dans l'Esprit peut signifier différentes choses. Cependant, une chose est certaine, il faut avoir l'Esprit pour prier en Esprit. Dans Jean 14: 16-17, Jésus a dit aux disciples qu'il prierait le Père et qu'il leur donnerait un autre consolateur, qui pourrait demeurer avec ses disciples pour toujours. En d'autres termes, l'Esprit de Vérité, que le monde ne peut pas recevoir, car il ne le voit pas, ni le connaît, mais ses disciples le connaissent, car il habite avec eux et sera en eux.

De plus, Romains 8: 9 a déclaré sans ambiguïté que quiconque n'a pas l'Esprit (Saint-Esprit) n'est pas le Sien. De plus, dans Jean 3: 5, Jésus a dit à Nicodème qu'il devait naître de l'eau et de l'Esprit pour entrer dans le royaume de Dieu. Deuxièmement, dans Jean 4: 23-24, Jésus dans sa conversation avec la Samaritaine au puits, lui a dit que le Père cherche à être adoré en Esprit et en vérité. De plus, parce que Dieu est un Esprit, ceux qui l'adorent doivent l'adorer en esprit et en vérité.

Pour tous ceux qui sont dirigés par l'Esprit de Dieu, ils sont les fils de Dieu …………… Car vous avez reçu l'Esprit d'adoption, par lequel vous criez Abba, Père. L'Esprit lui-même témoigne avec notre esprit, que nous sommes les enfants de Dieu. Romains 8:14, Romains 8:15, Galates 4: 5-6

De même, l'Esprit aide également nos maladies, car nous ne savons pas ce que nous devons prier comme nous le devrions, mais l'Esprit lui-même nous intercède avec des gémissements qui ne peuvent pas être prononcés. Et celui qui sonde les cœurs sait ce qu'est l'esprit de l'Esprit parce qu'il intercède pour les saints selon la volonté de Dieu (Romains 8: 26-27). Prier dans l'Esprit donne au croyant l'opportunité et l'accès au seul, qui peut fournir, bénir, guérir et sauver. Nous pouvons être assurés que Dieu non seulement entend, mais nous sommes convaincus qu'il répondra. Quelle que soit la réponse, que ce soit oui ou non, nous aurons sa paix.

Bien que ces cinq principes ne soient pas une application exhaustive de la prière, notre prière est que ces cinq principes vous aideront à établir une vie quotidienne de prière forte qui soit ancrée dans le cadre de la prière enseignée par les Écritures. Toute prière doit être faite avec foi envers Dieu, reconnaissant à qui vous priez. Toute prière doit reconnaître Jésus pour que le Père soit glorifié dans le Fils. Jean 14: 13-14 dit, tout ce que vous demanderez en mon nom, je le ferai, afin que le Père soit glorifié dans le Fils. Si vous demandez quelque chose en mon nom, je le ferai! La communication (prière) avec Dieu doit faire partie de notre style de vie. Nous devons donc nous engager quotidiennement dans la prière. Lorsqu'une personne communique, elle alterne entre écouter et parler. Il en va de même pour la prière, lorsque nous communiquons avec Dieu.

Lorsque vous priez, commencez par la louange tout en reconnaissant votre Père céleste. Deuxièmement, repentez-vous des péchés et / ou fautes connus et inconnus. Lorsque nous confessons nos péchés au Seigneur, notre avocat, nous prenons possession de nos actions tout en admettant notre besoin et notre dépendance à l'égard du Seigneur. Troisièmement, notre temps de prière devrait inclure des supplications pour les autres. Lorsque nous considérons le nombre de personnes que nous connaissons de nos proches, amis, connaissances, voisins, collègues, il y a beaucoup de gens et leurs besoins pour prier, en particulier pour leur salut. Quatrièmement, nous devons prier pour être utilisé comme témoin quotidiennement, en plus de prier pour nos besoins spécifiques et les domaines de notre vie dont nous avons besoin de l'aide du Seigneur. Enfin, nous devons exprimer notre gratitude au Seigneur avant de clore notre prière au nom de Jésus.

Ous serions négligents si nous ne partagions pas avec vous le message évangélique de la nouvelle naissance. Dans Jean chapitre 3, versets 1-8, Jésus a partagé le principe de la nouvelle naissance. Le disciple Luc nous a donné quatre témoins pour naître de nouveau; Actes 2: 37-39, Actes 8: 12-17, Actes 10.

Printed in the United States
By Bookmasters